WHAT'S YOUR VIEW?

PROTECTING SPECIES AND HABITATS

Sue Barraclough

FRANKLIN WATTS
LONDON•SYDNEY

First published in 2005 by
Franklin Watts
96 Leonard Street
London
EC2A 4XD

Franklin Watts Australia
Level 17/207 Kent Street
Sydney NSW 2000

© Franklin Watts 2005

ISBN: 0 7496 6307 3
Dewey decimal classification: 333.95

Series editor: Sarah Peutrill
Art director: Jonathan Hair
Design: Proof Books
Picture researcher: Sophie Hartley

Picture and text credits: see page 48.
Every attempt has been made to clear
copyright. Should there be any inadvertent
omission please apply to the publisher for
rectification.

Note on websites:
Every effort has been made by the Publishers
to ensure that the websites in this book
contain no inappropriate or offensive
material. However, because of the nature of
the Internet, it is impossible to guarantee
that the contents of these sites will not be
altered. We strongly advise that Internet
access is supervised by a responsible adult.

A CIP catalogue record for this book is
available from the British Library.

Printed in China

Contents

What's the issue?

For the human species, how best to protect other species and habitats is probably one of the most complex and difficult problems we face. Throughout the living world habitats are being destroyed and species are becoming extinct at an increasing rate. And one of the main difficulties seems to be that we cannot decide how important this is, or exactly what we can do.

WHAT IS IMPORTANT?

We might feel that our survival as a species is of the greatest importance and that there are species, and possibly habitats, that the world could afford to lose. But what about the bigger picture? Imagine living in a world that contains only humans, domestic pets and pests such as flies, mosquitoes and cockroaches.

Human activity and development, particularly agriculture and industry, have had a profound affect on ecosystems worldwide. We are using up the Earth's resources, and at the same time producing massive amounts of waste. Habitats from coral reefs to rainforests, mountains to deserts are being changed, and even destroyed, and many of the species that live there are struggling to survive. Campaigns to save popular species such as elephants, whales and apes will always find support but they can't be seen in isolation. Every species plays a role in its ecosystem and its extinction will have an effect on its habitat as a whole.

WHY DEBATE?

The fate of species and their habitats are closely intertwined and this book seeks to illustrate those connections and the human impact on them. We need to open up the debate and decide, globally and locally, how we should act for change. The facts and figures presented here will highlight some of the main issues and show the different, and complex, sides of the debates.

Most people agree that the elimination of global poverty and the promotion of sustainable development are both needed if we are to achieve a fair and peaceful world, and any effort to save species and habitats must take this into consideration. We all need to be aware of the extent to which we are harming and polluting our planet and, more importantly, that we can all do something about it.

Note on quotes

Quotes presented in this book in a specific context should not be understood to commit their source to one side of that debate. They are simply illustrations of the possible viewpoints in each debate.

People at a protest organised by Greenpeace – campaigners such as these take an active role in the environmental debate.

Q: Is the current rate of extinction part of the natural order?

EXTINCTION IS a natural event. Species disappear because they can't cope with climate changes, for example, or because another species competes for their food. Between one and ten species a year might vanish in this way. In the last 600 million years, however, there have been five mass extinctions – periods when over 60% of the Earth's species suddenly vanished. Many scientists believe that we are at the beginning of a sixth mass extinction – caused by humans through habitat destruction, over-hunting, pollution and climate change. The current rate of extinction may be thousands of times faster than the natural rate.

The dinosaurs are probably the most well known example of a mass extinction – and it was a result of natural causes.

YES 'Species naturally become extinct as they fail to reproduce, either through extreme conditions or because of displacement by competitors. Even if a species adapts to these threats, it will, by definition, have evolved into a different species.'
Richard Mackay, The Atlas of Endangered Species

'... catastrophes are always occurring in nature and on every scale of time and space, from a cold spring day that kills a fledgling robin to a glaciation that wipes out a species.'
Stephen Budiansky, Nature's Keepers

'In the natural environment species are constantly dying in competition with other species. It is estimated that more than 95% of all species that have ever existed are now extinct.'
Bjorn Lomborg, The Skeptical Environmentalist

✤ STATISTICALLY SPEAKING

The Living Planet Index (LPI) is an indicator of the world's biodiversity: it measures trends in the size of the populations of vertebrate species living on land, in freshwater, and in oceans around the world. The graph shows that the index fell by about 40% between 1970 and 2000. The data includes more than 1,100 species.

Source: The Living Planet Report, WWF

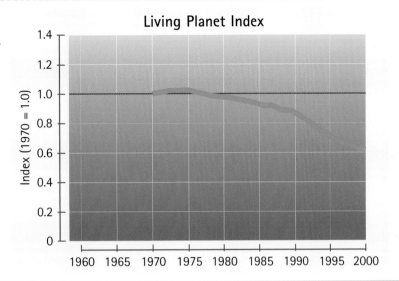

Living Planet Index

'We are in deep trouble biologically and already into a spasm of extinction of our own making unequalled since the one which took the dinosaurs ... The rate at which species disappear is about 1,000 to 10,000 times normal, and a quarter more of all species could vanish within a couple of decades.'

Tom Lovejoy, Reith Lecture

✖ 'The sixth extinction is not happening because of some external force ... it is happening because of us, *Homo sapiens*, an "exterminator species" as one scientist has characterised humankind.'

Stuart Pimm, conservation biologist

✖ 'It has been shown that the decimation of forests on one side of the world can have, sometimes devastating, climatic effects thousands of miles away in another continent. So we know that the greater the loss of animal and plant life, the more serious the consequences will be for mankind.'

Durrell Wildlife

✤ STATISTICALLY SPEAKING

• Before humans existed, the species extinction rate was (very roughly) one species per million species per year (0.0001%)

• Scientists estimate that approximately 137 species of life forms become extinct each day, and that works out at 50,000 per year.

MORE TO THINK ABOUT

It is difficult to assess accurately how much damage humans are doing to species because we have no clear idea as to how many species there actually are in the world. It is possible that many species will become extinct before we have even discovered them. Does that matter?

Q: Do we need biodiversity?

BIODIVERSITY is the web of living things – the differences between species and the many complex ways they interact with each other across a range of habitats. It gives us plants and animals for food, medicines and raw materials. Trees and other vegetation are crucial for climate stability and provide oxygen. Biodiversity is under threat due to habitat damage and change caused by pollution, urbanisation and farming. However, some scientists believe that we could live in a simplified world – we no longer need plants to make medicines, and genetic engineering and biotechnology can provide for our needs.

Can we survive without biodiversity, and would we want to?

YES

'In this age of biotechnology the countless millions of genes in the world's many millions of living creatures are surely among our greatest riches, to be compared with oil or precious metals.'
Colin Tudge, The Variety of Life

'The current decline in biodiversity is largely the result of human activity and represents a serious threat to human development.'
Chapter 15, Agenda 21, UN Department of Economic and Social Affairs

'What is man without the beasts? If all the beasts were gone, man would die from a great loneliness of spirit. For whatever happens to the beasts happens to man. All things are connected.'
Chief Seattle (19th Century Native American)

'The one ongoing process that will take millions of years to correct is the loss of genetic and species diversity by the destruction of natural habitats. This is the folly our descendants are least likely to forgive us.'
Dr Edward O Wilson, The Diversity of Life

NO '... Aldo Leopold, said, "The first rule of intelligent tinkering is to keep all the pieces." But I believe that we could live in a hugely impoverished world, and be clever enough to keep ourselves flourishing in it. It would be the world of the cult movie Blade Runner.'

Lord May, speaking at the Natural History Museum

✖ 'The benefits of biotechnology, today and in the future, are nearly limitless.'

Monsanto Biotech Primer

✖ '... unless a given element is identified as vital, it must have a finite value and there must therefore come a point at which the projected costs required to maintain it will outweigh any probable benefits.'

World Conservation Monitoring Centre

CASE STUDY

THE PACIFIC YEW

The Pacific Yew is a species of yew tree found in North America. Until the 1960s the tree was felt to have no practical use. Then scientists discovered that the bark contains a substance called Taxol, which they found could be used to treat some forms of cancer. Today the Pacific Yew is cultivated and Taxol can be made in laboratories using the trees' needles. Discoveries continue to be made about the uses for Taxol.

❈ STATISTICALLY SPEAKING

Results from National Survey on Biodiversity, USA
A survey of 1,500 adults

It is often not worth the cost in jobs to try to save endangered species, like spotted owls and snail darters.

The world would not suffer if some species, like poison ivy and mosquitoes, were eliminated.

There is so much land that is undeveloped, it is unlikely that we could do lasting damage to the Earth in our lifetimes.

We should loosen up environmental regulations on mining and drilling for oil in the USA because we need these resources for national security.

One of the most important things to me, in my life, is living in a world with a wide variety of plants and animals.

We do not need to worry so much about environmental problems because new technologies will help us solve most of them.

 Agree Disagree ▮ Don't know

MORE TO THINK ABOUT

Policies to maintain biodiversity are always going to be competing for funding that could be used to reduce poverty or improve healthcare and social services. Which is more important?

FIND OUT MORE: www.unep-wcmc.org/biodiversity www.foe.co.uk www.newscientist.com
www.un.org/esa/sustdev/agenda21 http://monsanto.co.uk/primer/primer.html

Q: Are we doing enough to save our forests?

FORESTS, especially rainforests, offer essential habitats for plants and wildlife, and are vital for regulating the climate, preventing soil erosion and storing water. Many people are concerned that logging is removing too much of this vital resource. However others say that the environmental impact is exaggerated and that many economies cannot afford to lose the revenues made from commercial logging.

YES

'We're continually growing more than we're cutting ... People think urban sprawl is eating all the forest – we can't say that.'

Brad Smith, an authority on the USA's estimated three billion trees at Forest Service headquarters in Arlington, Virginia

'We don't want our intentions bogged down by regulations. We want to get moving ... The new law directs courts to consider the long-term risks that could result if thinning projects are delayed.'

US President George W Bush, on a widely criticised law that opponents say will decrease the protection of forests

---

❖ STATISTICALLY SPEAKING

• The Forestry Stewardship Council (FSC) was set up to make sure that forests are managed in a sustainable way to internationally recognised standards.

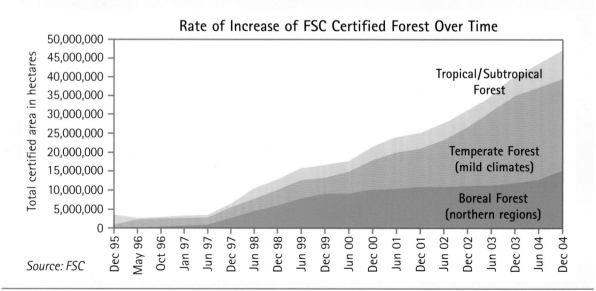

Rate of Increase of FSC Certified Forest Over Time

Total certified area in hectares

Tropical/Subtropical Forest

Temperate Forest (mild climates)

Boreal Forest (northern regions)

Source: FSC

NO 'Despite their importance for biodiversity and ecosystems, we are destroying forests at an unprecedented rate.'
Friends of the Earth

X 'Our comfy houses are contributing to the problem – in Europe, 50% of the tropical wood used in furniture, doors and window frames is logged illegally, often from irresponsibly managed ancient forests. This wood often fuels corruption and social conflict and destroys the homes of endangered or undiscovered species.'
Greenpeace International

CASE STUDY

AMAZON RAINFOREST – PARÁ

Around 40% of the world's tropical rainforest is found in the Amazon basin. Pará, the second largest Brazilian state, is the largest exporter of timber in the Amazon. An area of rainforest the size of Austria, the Netherlands, Portugal and Switzerland combined has been removed.

The landholders argue that logging creates jobs and contributes to the economy. They are asking the government to authorise new areas for logging. The federal and state governments are discussing this with them.

MORE TO THINK ABOUT

Each day, worldwide, the equivalent of 270,000 trees are flushed down the drain or end up in the dustbin. Producing and using paper products does not need to involve destroying forests. What do you think is needed to change this?

✱ STATISTICALLY SPEAKING

- 1 billion out of 1.2 billion people living in extreme poverty depend on forest resources for improving their livelihoods.
- We have lost 60% (some say 80%) of the forests that originally covered the Earth.
- Nearly 20% of the Amazon rainforest has been chopped down.

If burning forest for farming and road building is vital to the economy of a developing country, do we have a right to try to stop it?

FIND OUT MORE: www.panda.org/games/fsc www.itto.or.jp www.globalforestwatch.org http://forests.wri.org www.futureforests.com web.worldbank.org www.foe.org

Q: Can tourism help to protect species and habitats?

MANY TOURISTS are drawn to places where spectacular wildlife can be seen. So tourism can make a live whale or rhinoceros more valuable than a dead one. However, tourist companies have to ensure there is no damage to the environment that brought the tourists there in the first place. And although most holidaymakers agree that they don't want their holiday to cause damage to the environment, cost is still the most important factor in making their holiday choices.

NO

'At first glance, Ecuador's Galapagos Islands epitomise the promise of eco-tourism ... But closer examination reveals trade-offs: a flood of migrants seeking jobs in the islands' new tourist economy nearly tripled the area's permanent population over a 15-year period, turned the towns into sources of pollution, and added pressure to fishery resources.'
Martha Honey, author

✗ 'Sometimes as little as 10% of the money spent on a holiday remains in the destination economy.'
World Wildlife Fund

✗ 'Tourism is like fire. You can cook your supper with it, but it can also burn your house down.'
Anon, Asia

✗ 'More of us than ever before are venturing to the developing world. Places like Thailand, Egypt and South Africa with their diverse histories, cultures, breathtaking mountains, rivers and safari parks ... In fact, as we enjoy our well-earned breaks in the sun, we may not know whether the nearest villages have access to clean water, while our luxury western hotel boasts several swimming pools.'
Anita Roddick, founder of The Body Shop

Tourists relax by a pool at a hotel in Goa, India. Swimming pools can deprive the local environment and people of vital water supplies. Hotels also consume vast amounts of building materials and electricity, and create pollution and waste.

✖ 'Tourism is now one of the world's largest industries and one of its fastest growing economic sectors. The expected growth in the tourism sector and the increasing reliance of many developing countries, including small island developing states, on this sector as a major employer and contributor to local, national, sub-regional and regional economies highlights the need to pay special attention to the relationship between environmental conservation and protection and sustainable tourism.'

Agenda 21, Sustainable Tourism

CASE STUDY 1

IS IT ECO-TOURISM?

Belize, a small country in Central America, has managed to avoid the massive amount of development that dominates so much of Central America. Belize, as a very environmentally conscious country, has encouraged eco-tourism, however this is mainly run by foreign firms. This has meant that much of the profits of eco-tourism are leaving the country, and are not going towards conservation or local villagers. Furthermore in 1998, a Belize Department of Environment Report found that foreign-owned resorts and hotels were ignoring environmental laws and causing damage to coral reefs and fishing grounds.

Q: Can tourism help to protect species and habitats?

YES

'From African wildlife safaris, to diving tours in the Caribbean's emerald waters and coral reefs, to guided treks in Brazil's rainforests, nature-based tourism is booming ... This burgeoning interest in travelling to wild or untrammelled places may be good news, especially for developing countries. It offers a way to finance preservation of unique ecosystems with tourist and private-sector dollars and to provide economic opportunities for communities living near parks and protected areas.'

Wendy Vanasselt, World Resources Institute

'Travel is a natural right of all people and is a crucial ingredient of world peace and understanding.'

ASTA (American Society of Travel Agents)

'Tourism is number 1 in world trade. It is the largest export earner and employs millions of people around the world, directly or indirectly ... Tourism enriches individuals, families and entire communities – which would be so much poorer in spirit without the opportunities that tourism allows.'

World Tourism Organisation
Convention for Biological Diversity

'Antarctica belongs to the people of the world. The more people can see and experience it in an environmentally responsible way, the better chance it will be well managed for future generations.'

International Association of Antarctic Tour Operators

✿ STATISTICALLY SPEAKING

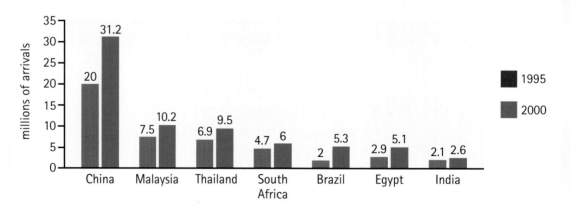

Number of tourist arrivals to some developing countries

millions of arrivals

	China	Malaysia	Thailand	South Africa	Brazil	Egypt	India
1995	20	7.5	6.9	4.7	2	2.9	2.1
2000	31.2	10.2	9.5	6	5.3	5.1	2.6

Source: Tearfunds World's Apart Tourism Report

✓ 'Tourism based on the natural environment (eco-tourism) is a vital growing segment of the tourism industry and, despite the negative impacts, and given the fact that tourism generates a large proportion of income and that a growing percentage of the activities are nature-based, tourism does present a significant potential for realising benefits in terms of the conservation of biological diversity.'

Convention for Biological Diversity

✓ 'Kenya earns the lion's share of its foreign currency, and of its national income, through tourism; and although the tourists come in part for the beaches they mainly come for the wildlife.'

Colin Tudge, The Variety of Life

A group of eco-tourists in Belize.

CASE STUDY 2

ADELIE PENGUINS

Adelie penguins are seen as one of the Antarctic's icons, but there has been a 40% decline in their numbers in the last two decades, and 21 colonies have become extinct.

Tourists to blame?

Some people are concerned that the Adelie penguins could be affected by the 4,300 tourists passing through their colonies each year. However, a study on Goudier Island found that tourists had no affect on the penguins. Declines may be due to increasing temperatures melting the ice. The lack of sea ice cover means there is less krill for the penguins to feed on.

MORE TO THINK ABOUT

One of the concerns about tourism is the environmental cost of flying. It's estimated that 60% of pollution caused by a holiday is due to the flight. Campaign groups say that aircraft emit more of the main greenhouse gases than cars for each passenger they carry. Should airlines, or passengers, be forced to pay towards the environmental cost?

FIND OUT MORE: www.astanet.com http://earthtrends.wri.org www.tearfund.org
www.world-tourism.org www.wttc.org

Q: Is exploiting the great apes the best way to save them?

In 20 years or so, this film of a mountain gorilla in Central Africa could be all we have left of one of our closest living relatives.

APES HAVE been used and exploited by humans throughout our history. The earliest use was as a food source, but more recently they have been exploited in medical research, as pets, and in films and TV. Despite efforts to conserve their habitat, deforestation is one of the biggest threats to apes. It's possible that exploiting them by encouraging high paying eco-tourists to visit the forests could be one way of preventing deforestation and saving the apes. However, while this kind of eco-tourism can help with conservation funding, it brings with it certain problems.

YES

'$25 million is the bare minimum we need, the equivalent of providing a dying man with bread and water. The clock is standing at one minute to midnight for the great apes, animals that share more than 96% of their DNA with humans. If we lose any great ape species we will be destroying a bridge to our origins, and with it part of our own humanity.'

Klaus Toepfer, UNEP Executive Director

'Tourism has been influential in helping to protect Rwanda's mountain gorillas and their habitat in Volcanoes National Park. Prior to the outbreak of civil war, tourist visits provided $1.02 million in direct annual revenues, enabling the government to create antipoaching patrols and employ local residents.'

Stefan Gossling, Ecotourism: A means to safeguard biodiversity and ecosystem function?

✿ STATISTICALLY SPEAKING

• It is believed that if we go on as we are then by 2030 the habitat left for ape populations will have declined to 10% of present levels in Africa and 1% in Southeast Asia.

• Some experts actually predict that gorillas, chimpanzees and orangutans will be extinct in the wild in 20 years.

Where are gorillas found?
There are two main species of gorilla. There are approximately 100,000 western gorillas (in two sub-species) located in West and Central Africa. The eastern gorilla includes three subspecies and is found in Rwanda, Uganda and the Democratic Republic of Congo. One of the eastern gorilla subspecies (the eastern lowland gorilla) numbers about 12,000, with very few in captivity. The other two subspecies – the Bwindi gorilla and the mountain gorilla – number some 350 each, with none in captivity.

Source: Dian Fossey Gorilla Fund

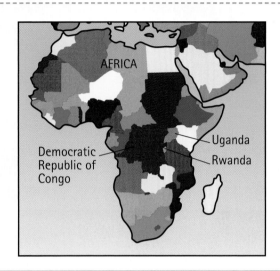

NO 'Stress to the animals can be provoked ... through regular contact with unfamiliar humans, which could potentially result in ... reduction in reproductive success.'

Liz Williamson, former director of Karisoke Research Centre

✗ 'Together with the high population pressure surrounding the parks, disease exposure ironically makes tourism one of the single greatest threats to mountain gorilla survival.'

Dr Jaco Homsy, in a report commissioned by the International Gorilla Conservation Programme

CASE STUDY

COLTAN
Most people have not heard of Coltan, but mobile phones cannot work without it. A Coltan mining boom in eastern Congo has caused the destruction of forests, and gorillas are killed to feed the miners and to sell at markets. Up to 90% of the eastern lowland gorillas may have been killed in the last three years alone.

MORE TO THINK ABOUT
What would happen if eco-tourism went out of fashion? If we exploit the apes in one way, how can we stop people exploiting them in another? Do attitudes need to change, should we care more whether the apes survive, without the need for exploitation?

Q: Should the worldwide ban on ivory trading be lifted?

IN 1986 ivory trading was banned worldwide, because elephant numbers were declining as a result of poaching. Today, in some parts of Africa, the populations of elephants have grown. They have a huge impact on their habitat, destroying trees and vegetation, and their numbers have to be controlled. The South African government argues that it can use money from ivory trading to guard against poaching, to buy land to extend the elephants' range and improve fencing. Many conservationists argue, however, that relaxing the ban would make policing the trade more difficult than it is now.

An African elephant in the wild.

YES

'More elephants have led to fewer trees [in West Africa's 'W' National Park], and this, combined with increased grass production as more sunlight penetrates once forested areas, has transformed a complex and varied riverine forest into a simplified grassland community. Birds and other species that once inhabited the forests along the river have disappeared.'

Caroline Taylor, The Challenge of African Elephant Conservation

'We must get this thing [proposal] approved ... If it does not happen, we will continue to try and convince people to support the proposal ... If someone wants to buy our ivory and burn it, we will sell it, because, believe you me, we need the money.'

Sanporus chief executive, Mavuso Msimang, on a proposal to sell two tonnes of ivory per year, from elephants that died naturally, in the Kruger National Park, South Africa. He proposed the money would be used to pay for elephant management and anti-poaching units

NO

'Ivory is not a product that people can eat or use for medicinal purposes. It's a product of vanity – made into necklaces or game boards, things where alternatives could be used ... The possibility of trade in ivory opening has already resulted in ivory stockpiling and illegal killing of elephants in various parts of Africa.'

Paula Kahumba (CITES coordinator for Kenya Wildlife Services)

✘ 'South Africa, Namibia and Botswana are some of the wealthiest countries in Africa and they have much more to offer than ivory.'

Daphne Sheldrick, founder of the David Sheldrick Wildlife Trust in Nairobi, Kenya

✘ 'The economics of ivory trade do not add up. Most countries where elephants live are poor and politically chaotic, and the effect of allowing even a limited trade would outweigh any benefits. Already struggling to protect their wildlife, these countries will be the first port of call for poachers, leading to increased costs in terms of both law enforcement and rangers' lives.'

Dr Richard Leakey, conservationist and politician

✿ STATISTICALLY SPEAKING

- Approximately 4,000 elephants a year are killed illegally for their ivory.

CASE STUDY

THE HISTORY OF IVORY

Ivory is a hard, usually creamy white, material that forms the tusks of elephants, and a few other mammals. In the past, ivory was taken from Indian, Burmese and African elephants, and later only from African elephants. Ivory has been widely used in Asia serving mainly as a material for objects of art.

In the 1970s, to protect endangered African elephant herds, an international treaty restricted the ivory trade. In 1989 more than 100 countries, including the USA, agreed to a complete ban.

A haul of elephant ivory, which had been illegally poached.

MORE TO THINK ABOUT

As long as there is a market for ivory, elephants are going to be killed for their tusks – should we tackle reducing the demand for ivory rather than the supply, and if so how?

FIND OUT MORE: www.bbc.co.uk/nature/animals/conservation/elephants
www.panda.org   www.traffic.org

Q: Can we justify the damage caused by intensive farming?

INTENSIVE FARMING means big fields, fewer types of crops, more machines and the application of artificial fertilisers and pesticides. For animal farmers it often means farming large numbers of one type of animal, keeping animals indoors and using drugs to prevent diseases.

Intensive farming has meant that today, fewer farmers feed more people, more cheaply than ever before. With the world's population continuing to grow we may need intensive farming to feed the world. However, some people believe that intensive farming methods, which use large amounts of fertiliser and pesticides, cause pollution and widespread damage to the environment.

These fields in Illinois, USA, show how vast areas of land are used for farming, wiping out habitats on a huge scale.

YES

'Without higher yields, the world would undoubtedly lose the wild forests and grasslands that still cover more than a third of the Earth's surface, because lower yield agriculture would require vastly more land. The demand will therefore be for more intensive agriculture embracing genetically modified crops.'

AstraZeneca International, biotechnology company

'Farming allows the UK to be 63% self-sufficient in all food and 74% self-sufficient in indigenous food ... The UK's picturesque countryside owes much to the generations of farmers and growers who have helped shape it over the years.'

National Farmers' Union, UK

'I don't deny that chemicals have brought some cost to the countryside ... But I'm afraid that we have to face up to reality here: everything we do that brings a benefit also brings a cost. We spend all our lives balancing benefits against costs, and farming is no different.'

Sean Rickard, former chief economist of the UK National Farmers' Union

'There is a need to double food production in developing countries, and, some 80% of this increase will need to be gained from land that is already under production. It is clear that this increased intensification of production cannot be met without chemical inputs.'

Louise O Fresco, Assistant Director-General, Agriculture Department and Agriculture Organisation of the United Nations

✪ STATISTICALLY SPEAKING

• This chart shows the growth of the world's population between 1800 and today, with a prediction for future growth until 2050.

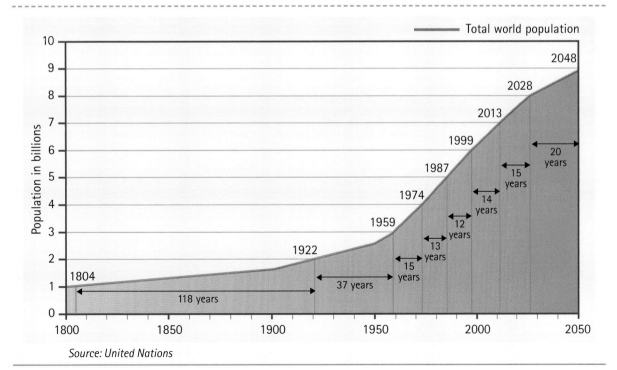

Source: United Nations

Q: Can we justify the damage caused by intensive farming?

NO 'To attempt to farm the whole Earth to feed people, even with organic farming, would make us like sailors who burnt the timbers and rigging of their ship to keep warm. The natural ecosystems of the Earth are not just there for us to take as farmland; they are there to sustain the climate and the chemistry of the planet.'

James Lovelock, scientist and environmentalist

❌ '... after driving a car, eating meat is alleged to be the most environmentally destructive thing you can do. The intensive farming of the global herd for meat and dairy causes deforestation, desertification and uses up precious land and water resources.'

Lucy Siegle, The Observer Magazine

❌ 'The farmers who have striven to raise their output of meat have in the main responded, as farmers in every age must always do, to the economic pressures of their day. The nutritionists who urged greater intake were sincere. Politicians concluded that the increase in livestock was good for people, and was in line with people's desires, and was also good for farmers and hence for the economy as a whole – and what else are politicians supposed to do? Yet the whole enterprise has been at least as damaging in the long term, as, say, the arms industry.'

Colin Tudge, So Shall We Reap

❌ 'All totalled, agriculture has displaced one-third of temperate and tropical forests and one-quarter of natural grasslands.'

Gregory Mock, World Resources

✳ STATISTICALLY SPEAKING

Water overuse is another major issue in today's farming. Large rivers such as the Nile, Yellow, and Colorado rivers, are often so depleted by withdrawals for agriculture that in dry periods they fail to reach the sea. Wetlands and inland water bodies dry up which has major consequences for species and habitats.

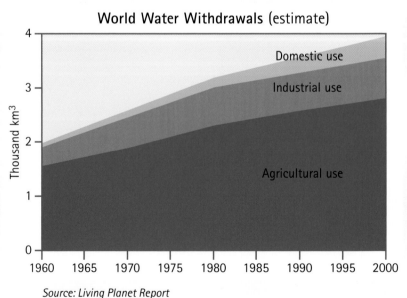

World Water Withdrawals (estimate)

Thousand km^3

Domestic use

Industrial use

Agricultural use

1960 1965 1970 1975 1980 1985 1990 1995 2000

Source: Living Planet Report

CASE STUDY

THE DEMAND FOR MEAT

Meat eating around the world is increasing at a massive rate. Since the 1960s consumption has grown from 56 to 89kg of meat per person, per annum (pp/pa) in Europe, and from 89 to 124kg in the USA. Similarly the Chinese were eating only 4kg of meat pp/pa in the 1960s. Now they eat 54kg pp/pa and consumption is still rising. Worldwide meat demand is expected to grow from 208 million tonnes in 1997 to 327 million tonnes in 2020.

Intensive meat farming

All this means that farming has to become more intensive to keep up with demand: requiring more land, more water, more energy and more chemicals. While soya beans yield 160kg of protein per acre and wheat 62kg, meat only yields 20kg. Furthermore the more meat we eat, the more grain, soya and other feedstuffs are needed to feed the animals. Approximately 70% of everything grown is used to feed animals, which are then killed to feed us.

MORE TO THINK ABOUT

There are many other issues surrounding intensive farming, for example you could investigate: fertilser and pesticide run-off, pest resistance, farmers' livelihoods, year-round availability of a variety of foods and new technologies.

❄ STATISTICALLY SPEAKING

• Agriculture accounts for almost 40% of land use and 25% of carbon dioxide production.

We farm animals, such as pigs, for meat in such huge numbers that the greenhouse gases they produce are a major contributor to global warming.

FIND OUT MORE: www.bbc.co.uk/nature/environment/conservationnow/global/agriculture
www.ciwf.org.uk/eatlessmeat

Q: Do the advantages of introducing alien species balance the costs?

Water hyacinths, brought in by accident from Latin America, have clogged up Lake Victoria in Uganda.

SINCE HUMANS started trading and travelling around the world they have taken animals and plants with them. Almost every part of the world has been affected by, and in many cases benefited from, the introduction of new species. However, sometimes these 'alien species', introduced either by accident or design, invade and disrupt natural ecosystems and are thought to be second only to habitat loss, as a threat to biodiversity worldwide.

YES

'Virtually everything down on the farm is an exotic: of all crops, only sunflowers, cranberries, and Jerusalem artichokes evolved in North America. Corn, soybeans, wheat, and cotton have been imported from some other land. Cattle came from Europe ... On occasion, alien species out compete and thus replace native ones, but in the vast majority of instances, newcomers contribute in the sense that they add to the species richness or diversity of local ecosystems.'
Mark Sagoff, University of Maryland School of Public Policy

'The histories of farming, horticulture, forestry and aquaculture are thick with new, exotic species joining or replacing old. In many places, introduced species are the main source of food ... New species have often been essential, useful or at least harmless.'
The Economist

'While recent attention has focused on the adverse impacts of introduced species – also known as alien species – species introductions are a valid means to improve production and economic benefits from fisheries and aquaculture.'
FIGIS – Fisheries Global Information System

✿ STATISTICALLY SPEAKING

- Up to 49% of the world's endangered species are thought to be threatened by introduced species.

- 10% of introduced species survive in a new environment and 10% of these become pests, meaning 1% of introduced species become pests.

Number of species introductions into inland waters by country

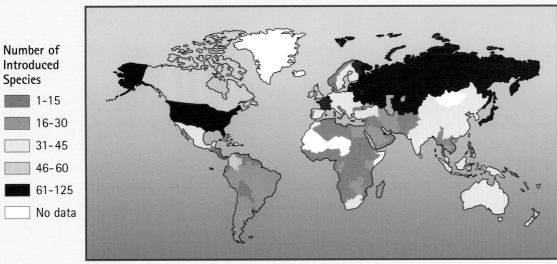

Number of Introduced Species

▨	1–15
▨	16–30
☐	31–45
▨	46–60
■	61–125
☐	No data

Source: Revenga et al

NO 'South Africa will need to spend about $900 million in the next 20 years to control invasive trees and plants that consume about 3.3 billion m³ of water annually.'
World Resources Institute

✗ '... moving goods around the world quickly provides the ideal opportunities for the accidental introduction of species ranging from zebra mussels to disease-carrying mosquitoes to bacteria and viruses ... When the costs have become apparent, they usually must be paid by someone other than those who sponsored or promoted the introduction – often the general public.'
Jeffrey McNeely, The World Conservation Union

✗ 'In Australia to control six weed species in agriculture costs US $105 million per year ... A sample of economic costs of damage from alien species of plants and animals is $137 billion per year.'
The World Conservation Union

MORE TO THINK ABOUT
On Ascension Island, cats were introduced to catch the rats that were accidentally introduced there. It backfired though, because the cats started killing the island's bird population instead.

FIND OUT MORE: www.iucn.org www.issg.org www.actionbioscience.org/environment
www.fao.org/fi http://earthtrends.wri.org

Q: Should cloning be used to save endangered species?

CLONING IS a way of taking the cells of a plant or animal and making another plant or animal that is exactly like it – in effect a copy. Since scientists cloned Dolly the sheep in 1996, the idea of cloning as a way to save endangered, even extinct, animal species has been taken up by a number of scientists worldwide. Many people are worried, however, that cloning may have irreversible effects with consequences as yet unknown.

Prometea (foreground), the world's first cloned horse, with the horse she was cloned from.

YES

'... there is reason to believe that cloning can assist in the preservation of genetic diversity in ... small populations. The cloned animals, as individuals, might serve as [a way to retain] genetic variation otherwise lost.'

Oliver A. Ryder, Trends in Biotechnology

'So this paves the way towards saving for instance the giant panda, the gorillas of East Africa, and even extinct species such as the bucado mountain goat.'

Dr Robert Lanza, pioneer of cloning technology

'This entire process has been a team effort. We are proud to have been part of this team that demonstrates the value of embryo technology as a tool that can be applied to endangered species management.'

Dr David Faber, president of Trans Ova Genetics, on an announcement that two banteng clones were born to Angus cows and were derived from cells of a male banteng that died 23 years earlier.

NO 'The cloning of species is as far removed from the spirit and psychology of conservation as we've ever been since man first noticed he was killing off the birds and beasts ... Cloning endangered species is a classic case of science no longer being used for prevention, but for apparent cure ... But what will we then do with these phoenix-like creatures? If their habitat is no more, where will we put them?'

Malcolm Tait, The Ecologist

'Just cloning one individual doesn't ensure that you've got the kind of genetic variation in the population that you need to sustain it.'

Michael Novacek, leader of the effort at the American Museum of Natural History in New York, USA, to collect genetic material from endangered species

'We spend millions of rupees trying to clone cheetahs and lions but where will we put them? We are losing forests thanks to highways and road projects and poachers are killing our tiger population. Cheetahs need antelope to eat and space to hunt. We do not have enough of either ... The government has big hopes of biotechnology in India. This is really about science rather than conservation.'

Belinda Wright, Wildlife Protection Society of India, commenting on the Indian government's plans to use cloning technology to save India's lion population and return Asiatic cheetahs to the wild

✳ STATISTICALLY SPEAKING

'As you may know, scientists have made advances in cloning, where they can reproduce a whole animal from a single cell. Do you think it is acceptable to use cloning to...' (see below)	Acceptable %	Not Acceptable %	Don't know %
reproduce endangered species?	29	64	7
reproduce livestock?	23	71	6
reintroduce extinct species?	20	72	8
reproduce a beloved pet such as a dog or cat?	12	84	4
reproduce humans?	7	89	4

Source: FOX News/Opinion Dynamics Poll

MORE TO THINK ABOUT

Some scientists predict that in the future techniques for cloning endangered species could become cheaper to implement than more traditional means of preservation, such as breeding and habitat protection programmes. Do you think this would be a good idea?

27

Q: Do zoos help to protect species?

Many people are uncomfortable with images of wild animals behind bars.

ZOOS AND wildlife parks are generally not set up for conservation purposes – they are usually intended for education and profit. And while many zoos have breeding programmes for endangered species, some people argue that these do little for actual conservation and that putting animals in cages is not protection at all. However, if zoos did not exist, even more species would have died out completely by now. Furthermore, money made by captive-breeding schemes can be used to pay for conservation in the wild.

NO 'The central focus of zoos is not the care of wild animals; it is to expand their overly inflated budgets, minimise knowledge of their inhumane methods of operation, and maintain public support for their continued existence.'
NOAZ – National Organisation to Abolish Zoos

✘ 'Conservation of animals in their natural habitat is clearly preferable, since it enables the animals to live a natural, and in many cases social, existence.'
Richard Mackay, The Atlas of Endangered Species

✘ 'You only have to look at a bird in a cage and ask the question, "Why do birds have wings?" The rest follows.'
Virginia McKenna, actress in Born Free

✘ 'If the only tigers left in the world were in zoos would tigers have any point at all? ... All captive-breeding schemes ... are a drop in the ocean; hopeless gestures.'
Colin Tudge, The Variety of Life

✷ STATISTICALLY SPEAKING
• Only 5% of animals kept in zoos are 'endangered'.

YES 'For many wildlife species, from cheer pheasants to oryx, captive breeding is helpful, sometimes essential, if the species are to survive. Captive breeding has too many success stories to be dismissed out of hand ... For the big animals, the sexy animals, the popular animals, the appealing animals, and even for a few that were just plain fortunate, captive breeding has worked.'

B. K. Mackay, When Captive Breeding Works

'For an alarmingly large number of animal, and even plant, species, whose numbers have dwindled drastically, captive breeding remains the only hope.'

World Wildlife Fund

'The Wildlife Conservation Society saves wildlife and wild lands. We do so through careful science, international conservation, education, and the management of the world's largest system of urban wildlife parks, led by the flagship Bronx Zoo. Together, these activities change individual attitudes toward nature and help people imagine wildlife and humans living in sustainable interaction on both a local and a global scale.'

Wildlife Conservation Society

✪ STATISTICALLY SPEAKING

• The minimum number for a viable, self-sustaining population is thought to be 500.

CASE STUDY

THE MALLORCAN MIDWIFE TOAD

The Durrell Wildlife Trust has successfully run a captive breeding campaign to save the Mallorcan Midwife Toad. It was thought to be extinct until 1980, when several live adult toads were found. The Trust set up a captive-breeding scheme and toads were first reintroduced to the wild in 1989. Since then hundreds of toads and tadpoles have been released into the wild. It is now listed as vulnerable rather than critically endangered, so its future is looking brighter.

MORE TO THINK ABOUT

Zoos generally breed from the animals in a species best able to cope with being in a zoo – those that are less fierce and wild – so these species will begin to change, as cows and dogs have done. It is also widely believed that for best results, breeding must be done with minimum human contact – do you think this is a good reason to use these methods? Tigers are endangered in the wild, however, and captive breeding has been so successful that zoos worldwide have too many of them.

Q: Is global warming a major threat?

THE ISSUE of global warming and climate change is hugely controversial. Carbon dioxide and other greenhouse gases are generally accepted to be responsible for changes to the characteristics of the Earth's atmosphere, leading to global warming. Some scientists think this will have a massive effect on the world's habitats through rising sea levels and changing climates. However other scientists believe that the effects are exaggerated and that some of the changes are caused by natural phenomena over which we have no control.

YES

'Forests are highly sensitive to climate change and up to one third of currently forested areas could be affected by climate change in some way, according to the Intergovernmental Panel on Climate Change (a group of more than 2,500 of the world's leading scientists). Global warming poses myriad threats to the survival of rainforests. Warmer temperatures and changing rainfall patterns may create the conditions for increased forest fires. In addition, as global temperatures rise, tree species may not be able to shift their range fast enough to survive.'

BBC Science & Nature website

'Global warming is the single biggest environmental problem this world faces.'

Valli Moosa, president of the World Conservation Union

Some scientists think that declines in the numbers of Adelie penguins is due to rising temperatures melting the ice. The lack of sea ice cover means there is less krill for the penguins to feed on (see page 15).

✱ STATISTICALLY SPEAKING

Average temperature of the Earth's surface

late 1800s: 3.8°C   Today: 4.4°C   Future estimate: 5.8°C by the year 2100

Sea levels:

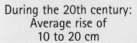

During the 20th century: Average rise of 10 to 20 cm

Future estimate by UN: 9 to 88 cm rise by the year 2100

NO 'If our goal is to improve the world, reducing carbon emissions is most certainly not the most effective way ... for the same amount that implementing Kyoto will cost the EU every year, the UN estimates that we could provide every person in the world with access to basic health, education, family planning and water and sanitation services. Wouldn't this be a better way of serving the world?'

Bjorn Lomborg, The Skeptical Environmentalist

CASE STUDY

KYOTO PROTOCOL

The 1997 Kyoto Protocol aims to reduce world CO_2 emissions. However, some scientists are concerned that it won't work unless all the world's governments sign up. The USA has not signed up to the Kyoto Protocol as they have concerns about its effect on US industry and employment. The USA produces 25% of the world's greenhouse gas emissions while they make up only 4% of the world's population. On the other hand, the USA and other industrialised countries produce most clean technologies.

✖ 'The whole tissue of argument that makes climate change the greatest problem facing humanity is based on a long series of improbabilities.'

Myron Ebell, Washington think-tank official

✖ 'We do not know how much effect natural fluctuations in climate may have had on warming. We do not know how much our climate could, or will change in the future ... no one can say with any certainty what constitutes a dangerous level of warming ...'

George W Bush, US President

MORE TO THINK ABOUT

No one can be sure if and when climate change will have a major effect on the Earth's habitats. If big changes might not occur for a few hundred years should we be concerned about the possible effect on the generations of the future, when there are clearly problems in the world that need to be dealt with today?

FIND OUT MORE: www.co2.org www.visitandlearn.co.uk
www.newscientist.com www.peopleandplanet.net

Q: Should developing countries adopt sustainable development?

An organic flower farm. Is eco-agriculture the answer to reducing poverty and saving biodiversity?

THE AIM of sustainable development is to find ways of providing for our needs – energy, water, fuels, foods – using methods that are not at the expense of future generations. Many scientists argue that if industry and agriculture carry on as they are now, destroying habitats, using up resources and polluting the planet, the world's species do not have a viable chance of surviving. But should the world's developing countries be expected to grow sustainably as they try to reduce poverty and catch up with the rest of the world?

YES

'The elimination of global poverty and the promotion of sustainable development are essential to a fair and equitable world. The current patterns of consumption and production are among the major causes of the degradation of the Earth's resources.'

The Network of Women Ministers of the Environment

'Endangered species, essential farmlands and desperately poor humans often occupy the same ground ... The report calls for a new approach to protecting biodiversity which combines conservation and farming efforts ... Examples include planting windbreaks to connect patches of forest, and growing trees on pasturelands to protect forest birds and shade coffee plantations. In many cases, bringing nature back to the fields has boosted productivity by attracting pollinators, improving soils and providing new crops such as fruit, medicinal plants and fodder.'

Fred Pearce, New Scientist

✿ STATISTICALLY SPEAKING

- Three billion people, that is half the world's population, live on less than $2 a day.

The ecological footprint is the area of land required to sustain an individual or population. On the chart, the height of each bar represents each region's average footprint per person, the width is proportional to its population and the area of the bar represents the region's total ecological footprint.

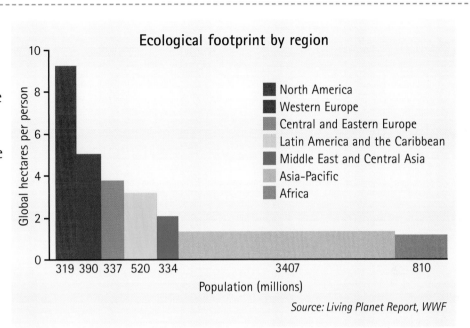

Ecological footprint by region

■ North America
■ Western Europe
■ Central and Eastern Europe
□ Latin America and the Caribbean
■ Middle East and Central Asia
■ Asia-Pacific
■ Africa

Y-axis: Global hectares per person (0 to 10)
X-axis: Population (millions) — 319 390 337 520 334 3407 810

Source: Living Planet Report, WWF

NO '...we have become so preoccupied with worrying about small problems for future generations in rich countries that the much greater needs of the poor now have been neglected.'

Bjorn Lomborg, The Skeptical Environmentalist

✗ 'It is time to move beyond the phrase sustainable development into more specific actions dealing with sustainable energy, sustainable agriculture and sustainable use of water resources.'

Nitin Desai, UN secretary-general of the Johannesburg Summit

CASE STUDY

MYERS' RESERVES

Ecologist Norman Myers suggested a plan to preserve 25 areas of the world which would 'go far to stem the mass extinction of species'. But the scheme was controversial. These areas are home to up to a billion of the world's poorest people who need the land for farming. In 19 of the biodiversity hotspots, the population is growing more rapidly than in the world as a whole.

MORE TO THINK ABOUT

If you were poor and hungry would you care that your country was not developing sustainably?

FIND OUT MORE: www.oneworld.net www.newscientist.com
www.futureharvest.org

Q: Is a global plan the answer?

In 1992, the United Nations Conference on Environment and Development (UNCED) took place in Rio de Janeiro in Brazil. It became known as the Earth Summit. With 178 of the world's leaders attending, one of the aims was to agree on shared goals and to come up with a global plan for sustainable development. Many people feel that global action is too unwieldy and, for all the talking and planning, little has changed since 1992.

YES

'A summit provides focus for an issue. It forces an agenda. It persuades, cajoles and embarrasses governments into commitments.'
Tony Blair, British Prime Minister

'The numbers of species ... and the extent of the relatively intact ecosystems that still exist in 100 years will be the greatest if we can find the means and the will to commit ourselves and our nations to the goal of global sustainability.'
Professor P Raven, director of the Missouri Botanical Garden

'While working for environmental protection at the local level, you can't ignore the global roots of local crises.'
Vandana Shiva, environmentalist and activist

A BRIEF HISTORY OF TALKS

Summit	Goals, plans and outcomes
1972 United Nations Conference on Human Environment, Sweden	The main aim was to come up with a global plan for change. The principles established here inspired many of the environmental laws that came later.
1985 Montreal Protocol, Canada	To reduce ozone depletion – targeting CFCs – and it was largely successful.
1987 World Commission on Environment and Development	Recommended that an international conference on environment and development should take place. This led directly to UNCED in 1992.
1992 United Nations Conference on Environment and Development (UNCED), Rio de Janeiro, Brazil	Conventions on Climate Change and Biodiversity. Outcome: Agenda 21, a 40 chapter action plan for sustainable development – the global plan would be broken down into achievable local actions.
1997 Kyoto Protocol, Japan	To combat climate change by reducing carbon emissions.
2002 United Nations World Summit on Sustainable Development (WSSD), Johannesburg, South Africa	To re-energise the global community to put into action the Rio agreements. It generated less enthusiasm than Rio. Outcomes: the Johannesburg Declaration on Sustainable Development and the Plan of Implementation that identified five areas of priority – water, energy, health, agriculture and biodiversity.

NO 'Governments' failure to agree on effective means of implementation (including financing) makes it likely that the success of WSSD [World Summit on Sustainable Development] could be rendered meaningless. Division within and between civil society and governments will remain an obstacle to addressing development and environment concerns for years or even decades to come.'

Antonio La Vina, Gretchen Hoff and Anne Marie De Rose, Earth Trends

✗ 'How many more decades must it take, lumbering incoherently from one summit to the next, to confront the core reality that our economies either develop sustainably, or they won't be developing at all.'

Jonathan Porritt, UK Sustainable Development Commission and Programme

Children gather under the Tree of Life at the Rio Earth Summit in 1992. We all share a common future, but are we any nearer to a sustainable one?

MORE TO THINK ABOUT

World summits, with their great plans for the future are really for the benefit of generations to come. With this in mind, in recent years 'Children's summits' have been launched, but many people think that these are not enough. They say learning about our common future needs to be as important in school education as studying our past. Do you think education could be more important than global agreements?

FIND OUT MORE: www.peacechild.org/bethechange
www.un.org/esa/sustdev www.iucn.org/wssd www.global-vision.org

Q: Would allowing whaling mean bigger catches for fishermen?

AN INTERNATIONAL whaling ban came into force in 1986 to protect endangered whale species and because the methods of killing them were thought to be inhumane. Some governments now say, however, that whales compete with humans for fish and that populations should be controlled. Others believe that the solution is to build up fish stocks by stopping overfishing, protecting habitats and creating protected areas and no-take zones.

Is overfishing by huge trawlers a more likely cause of dwindling fish stocks than too many whales?

YES

'The annual consumption of fish, krill and other biomass by whales in this region has been estimated around 6 million metric tons, several times the total Icelandic fishery landings of 1.5 to 2.0 million metric tons. This is an indication of the impact that whales are having on the marine ecosystem.'

Sverrir Haukur Gunnlaugsson, Ambassador, Embassy of Iceland

'We cannot adopt a laissez-faire attitude towards management of whale stocks; our fisheries are being seriously damaged as increasing whale populations feed on many economically-important fish species.'

Joji Morishita, Japanese Government

❋ STATISTICALLY SPEAKING

• Estimates put the amount of fish eaten by marine mammals worldwide at more than 800 million tonnes annually, or roughly 10 times the worldwide ocean fish harvest.

NO 'Huge modern fishing fleets can threaten the entire ocean food chain. Fishing vessels drag large nets or scoops across the ocean floor to gather prawns, scallops and fish such as cod and haddock ... In some waters, fishing is so intensive that each hectare of seabed is on average trawled in its entirety seven times a year.'

BBC Science & Nature Website – Eco Top Ten Marine

✗ 'Fishers accuse whales and seals of eating their precious, diminishing fish stocks, leading to renewed calls that these mammals be culled to safeguard the future of a beleaguered industry. Conservationists and animal welfare advocates retort that it is the other way round ... overfishing is taking food from the mouths of some of the world's most endangered animals, stifling their recovery. The first global study of its kind ... shows that marine mammals and fishing fleets rarely prey heavily on the same fish stocks.'

Bob Holmes, New Scientist Online

✤ STATISTICALLY SPEAKING

• About 95% of marine life caught by a typical shrimp trawler dies on deck and is discarded. • The oceans provide 15% of the animal protein people eat.

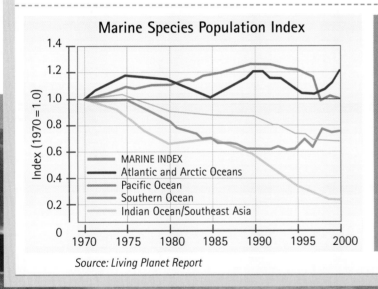

Marine Species Population Index

Index (1970 = 1.0)

MARINE INDEX
Atlantic and Arctic Oceans
Pacific Ocean
Southern Ocean
Indian Ocean/Southeast Asia

Source: Living Planet Report

MORE TO THINK ABOUT

In many countries whales are well-loved. However, if populations are improving, is killing them for food any different to other animals? After all, they have been used in the Japanese diet for many years.

Do images like this give us an over-romantic view of whales?

FIND OUT MORE: www.greenpeace.org.uk/oceans www.earthwatch.unep.net/oceans
www.whaling.jp/english/qa/html www.iwcoffice.org/

Q: Will creating coral reef reserves protect them?

Coral reefs are rich in biodiversity.

CORAL REEFS provide habitats for a large variety of organisms and may be vital to the stability of our oceans. They are damaged by tourism directly through diving and boating and indirectly by the construction and operation of tourism infrastructure (resorts, marinas, etc). Many governments try to protect coral reefs by creating reserves – Australia's Great Barrier Reef shows the potential of careful management. However, many scientists believe that coral reefs are more seriously in danger from other factors such as climate change, overfishing and pollution from industry and agriculture.

YES

'No-take reserves have been scientifically shown to increase the size, number and variety of fish while allowing damaged ecosystems to recover.'

David White, Director of Ocean Conservancy's Florida office

'Even though nearly two thirds of coral reefs are now officially endangered, some are bouncing back despite warmer oceans and pollution, giving hope the marine marvels are not completely doomed.'

Ed Cropley, Reuters

' ... diving, well planned, can add value to the reefs for local people and promote conservation. Tourism can become a force for good ... often providing a direct income ... for the management of marine protected areas.'

The World Atlas of Coral Reefs

✪ STATISTICALLY SPEAKING

• More than 30% of the world's corals have been lost and the remainder are increasingly threatened, along with the countless species that live in them.

NO '... coral reefs are threatened the world over, despite the committed efforts of individuals and groups to save these fragile and valuable ecosystems. In the past two decades, human activities have continued to destroy coral reefs through sedimentation, coastal development, destructive fishing practices and pollution.'

ICRAN (International Coral Reef Action Network)

✖ '... a panel of the world's most eminent coral reef scientists issued a stark warning that illustrated just how widespread the effects of climate change will be. Among its many other negative effects, they warned, will be the death of coral reefs all over the world as a result of warming seas.'

Caspar Henderson, The Ecologist

✖ 'Coral reefs are under assault, they are rapidly being degraded by human activities. They are over-fished, bombed and poisoned. They are smothered by sediment, and choked by algae growing on nutrient rich sewage and fertiliser run-off. They are damaged by irresponsible tourism and are being severely stressed by the warming of the world's oceans. Each of these pressures is bad enough in itself, but together, the cocktail is proving lethal.'

Klaus Toepfer, UNEP Executive Director

❉ STATISTICALLY SPEAKING

• It is estimated that up to 80% of the world's protected areas are protected in name only and are not actively managed at all.

❉ STATISTICALLY SPEAKING

The table shows the various levels of risk to coral reefs from different sources.

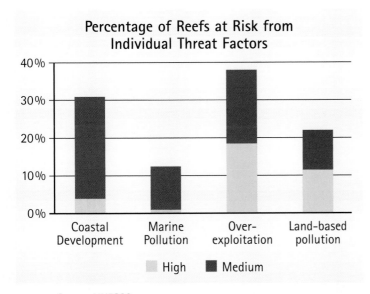

Percentage of Reefs at Risk from Individual Threat Factors

High   Medium

Source: UNESCO

MORE TO THINK ABOUT

If countries lose revenue from tourism, will this lead to conservation loss in other areas? How important is conservation of the oceans? Currently 12% of land is under conservation, but only 1% of the oceans.

FIND OUT MORE: www.icran.org   www.earthdive.com   www.panda.org
www.greenpeace.org   www.earthwatch.unep.net/oceans

Q: Do the benefits of dams outweigh the environmental cost?

DAMS HAVE been built for thousands of years to control and make good use of water sources – the reservoirs they create help governments to ensure a clean water supply and to irrigate land. Dams can help to control flooding and can also be used to provide hydroelectric power. However, building a large-scale dam is hugely expensive, destroys habitats in the immediate area and also has knock-on effects for habitats further down the river and beyond.

YES

'[blocking the Yangtze River is a] remarkable feat in the history of mankind to reshape and exploit natural resources.'
China's President Jiang Zemin, on a step forward in the construction of the controversial Three Gorges Dam

'Hydropower is America's leading source of clean, renewable energy.'
Hydro Research Foundation

'[Dams] improve water supply ... provide power, mitigate floods, and reduce fossil fuel depletion and the environmental effects of fossil fuel burning ... The World Bank adopts a set of safeguard polices to ensure that dams are economically well justified and environmentally and socially sound.'
The World Bank Group

✱ STATISTICALLY SPEAKING

• Hydropower plants produce about 20% of the world's electricity. The energy output of the world's hydropower plants is the equivalent of 3.6 billion barrels of oil.

The Glen Canyon hydroelectric dam in Utah, USA – clean energy supplier or habitat destroyer?

NO

'Big dams are horrible things. They flood wide areas, drowning wildlife and displacing thousands of people.'

James Wolfensohn, The Economist

'The plan to build a dam and donate revenue to the environment has drawn controversy in past decades, as the proposed dam would flood 450 square kilometres in the heart of the conservation area. In addition to the nearly 400 Asian elephants at risk, the project would affect a number of species on the IUCN's endangered "Red List", including the rare white-winged duck.'

Probe International on the Nam Theun 2 dam project in Laos

✱ STATISTICALLY SPEAKING

• Dams have altered the flow of approximately 60% of the world's major river basins, affecting many species.

'... it is clear that large dams have led to the loss of forests and wildlife habitat, the loss of species populations ... the loss of aquatic biodiversity, and of upstream and downstream fisheries, and of the services of downstream floodplains, wetlands, and riverine, estuarine and adjacent marine ecosystems ...'

World Commission on Dams

✱ STATISTICALLY SPEAKING

• There are more than 45,000 large dams in the world, most of them built in the last 35 years.

CASE STUDY

THE THREE GORGES DAM

The Three Gorges Dam on the Yangtze River in China, if completed, will be the largest hydroelectric dam in the world. Once built, its reservoir will stretch over 560 square kilometres, water pollution and deforestation will increase, the shoreline will be eroded and the altered ecosystem will further endanger many species.

However, Chinese officials say the dam may end up providing as much as 11% of the nation's electricity. Considering that China burns 50 million tonnes of coal each year for energy, their point is that the environmental benefits outweigh the environmental damage.

MORE TO THINK ABOUT

You could look into the effects of other big dams, for example:
Aswan High Dam (Egypt)
Edwards Dam (USA)
Folsom Dam (USA)
Grand Coulee Dam (USA)
Hoover Dam (USA)
Itaipu Dam (Brazil and Paraguay)
South Fork Dam (USA)

FIND OUT MORE: www.irn.org   www.dams.org/
www.worldbank.org/water

Q: Does our survival depend on the well-being of the Earth?

THROUGH AGRICULTURE and industry the human species has been able to ignore the limitations of natural ecosystems, and largely disregard the delicate balance of nature. Many people believe that we are destroying the planet and that we have too little understanding of how complex ecosystems work and how our actions affect them to continue to disregard natural laws in this way. However, many scientists argue that we are intelligent enough to survive independently of the natural world.

YES

'When man continues to destroy nature, he saws off the very branch on which he sits. The rational protection of nature is – at the same time – the protection of mankind.'
Gerald Durrell, author and conservationist

'Conflicts are waged over resources such as land, forests, minerals, oil and water ... Protecting local and global environments is therefore essential for achieving lasting peace. It is critical that people around the world take action to reverse environmental degradation and its negative impacts on our lives and on other species.'
Professor Wangari Maathai, winner of Nobel Peace Prize

'Treat the Earth well. It is not given to you by your parents. It was loaned to you by your children.'
Kenyan proverb

'Knowledge is power. We can be the masters of our destiny.'

Francis Bacon, philosopher 1561-1626

'Space is about the present as well as the future of the human species ... It is about the wellbeing of the present generation, as well as opportunities and hopes of future generations. It holds vast potential to help humanity meet its growing needs ... People are destined to travel into space, engage in increased economic activities in space, and some day establish settlements in space.'

American Astronautical Society

CASE STUDY

BIOSPHERE TWO

The Biosphere Two experiment took place in Arizona, USA, from 1991 to 1993. Some 3,800 species and eight humans were housed in a vast greenhouse. The idea was to start afresh and create a sustainable environment, sealed off from the rest of the world. The project's aim was to create a natural, balanced ecosystem in which people and nature could live in harmony. The project failed miserably. In less than a year, 19 of the 25 species of vertebrate animals had died. All the insect pollinators died too, so it was only a matter of time before the plants died. Most worryingly of all, scientists do not understand exactly why the project was such a disaster.

MORE TO THINK ABOUT

Scientists say that since the mid-1980s, because of the rate we have consumed and thrown resources away, we have exceeded nature's ability to regenerate. What sort of lives should we want – is it natural to live for today only?

FIND OUT MORE: www.astronautical.org www.fauna-flora.org
www.rootsandshoots.org www.worldwatch.org

Glossary

Agenda 21 a non-legally binding programme of action for sustainable development. It is made up of 40 chapters to guide governments on environmental and developmental issues. It was adopted by the 1992 United Nations Conference on Environment and Development at Rio de Janeiro.

Alien species also known as invasive, introduced, or non-native species.

Banteng a wild cattle species.

Biodiversity biodiversity or biological diversity is all of the differences between species and between individuals and the many complex ways they interact with each other across a range of habitats.

Biosphere the part of the Earth that can sustain life – all of the planet's ecosystems.

Biotechnology the use of living things to make products for human use.

Carrying capacity the population of a species that can be supported by a region without damaging the ecosystem.

Clone an organism that is genetically identical to its parent.

Commission a group of people who are given the task of investigating something.

Deforestation clearing an area of forest to be used for another purpose such as agriculture or tree plantations.

Developed countries richer countries that rely on industry (for example the UK, the USA, Japan).

Developing countries poorer countries that are trying to industrialise (like many in Africa, South America and Southeast Asia).

Ecological footprint the area of the Earth's surface required to support an individual or population.

Ecology the study of relationships between living things and their environment.

Ecosystem complex web of connections between living things and their environment.

Eco-tourism travel to places of great natural beauty or interest with the aim of not damaging them and contributing to their preservation.

Endangered species animals or plants that are in danger of dying out.

Environmentalist a person who is concerned about and wants to protect the environment.

Extinction the death of the last member of a species so that species no longer exists.

Genes a unit of heredity found in all living things, which is passed from parents to their offspring and will determine a characteristic of the offspring.

Genetic engineering technology used to make changes to genetic material.

Genetics the study of genes.

Global warming a gradual increase over time of the average temperature near the Earth's surface. Many scientists believe global warming is caused by greenhouse gases such as CFCs (chloro-fluorocarbons) and CO_2 (carbon dioxide).

Habitat the natural home of a living thing.

Intensive agriculture farming methods that seek to maximise production through the use of machinery, fertilisers and pesticides.

Pesticide a chemical used on crops to repel or kill insects and pests.

Protocol an agreement setting out the guidelines for the ways countries expect each other to behave with regard to a particular issue.

Species a group of similar living organisms that are able to breed with each other to produce fertile offspring. A keystone species is one that plays a crucial role in the ecosystem.

Summit a meeting between heads of two or more governments.

Sustainable development development that meets the needs of the present without compromising the ability of future generations to meet their needs.

Urbanisation the process by which a place becomes a town or city.

IMPORTANT ORGANISATIONS

These are a few of the major organisations mentioned in this book.

CITES: www.cites.org
The Convention on International Trade in Endangered Species of Wild Fauna and Flora came into force in 1975 after a meeting of 80 member countries of the IUCN. It aims to ensure that trade in wild animals and plants does not threaten their survival. Today, over 160 countries have signed up to CITES.

IUCN: www.iucn.org
The International Union for the Conservation of Nature and Natural Resource, commonly known as the World Conservation Union. It was founded in 1948 and is today the world's largest conservation organisation. It supports research into conservation and the sustainable management of natural resources.

UNEP: www.unep.org
The United Nations Environment Programme was set up in 1972 to provide a voice for environmental issues within the United Nations. It aims to educate and inform on a broad range of sustainable development and conservation issues.

World Bank: www.worldbank.org
An agency of the United Nations with 184 member countries. It aims to combat poverty by offering assistance through low interest loans and grants to the governments of developing countries to protect the environment, fight disease, build schools and provide clean water and energy. The money for these grants comes from the world's 40 or so wealthiest nations who make contributions every four years.

WWF: www.worldwildlife.org
Established in 1961 as the World Wildlife Fund, WWF is one of the world's biggest conservation organisations, providing funding for almost 2,000 projects in 100 countries across the world. It is involved in everything from climate change to preserving individual species and sustainable agriculture.

Debating tips

WHAT IS DEBATING?

A debate is a structured argument. Two teams speak in turn for or against a particular question. Usually each person is given a time they are allowed to speak for and any remarks from the other side are controlled. The subject of the debate is often already decided so you may find yourself having to support opinions with which you do not normally agree. You may also have to argue as part of a team, being careful not to contradict what others on your side have said.

After both sides have had their say, and had a chance to answer the opposition, the audience votes for the side they agree with.

DEBATING SKILLS

1 Know your subject

Research it as much as you can. The debates in this book give opinions as a starting point, but there are website suggestions for you to find out more. Use facts and information to support your points.

2 Make notes

Write down key words and phrases on cards. Try not to read a prepared speech. You might end up losing your way and stuttering.

3 Watch the time

You may be given a set amount of time for your presentation, so stick to it.

4 Practise how you sound

Try to sound natural. Think about:
Speed – Speak clearly and steadily. Try to talk at a pace that is fast enough to sound intelligent and allows you time to say what you want, but slow enough to be understood.
Tone – Varying the tone of your voice will make you sound interesting.
Volume – Speak at a level at which everyone in the room can comfortably hear you. Shouting does not win debates. Variation of volume (particularly speaking more quietly at certain points) can help you to emphasise important points but the audience must still be able to hear you.
Don't ramble – Short, clear sentences work well and are easier to understand.

GET INVOLVED - NATIONAL DEBATING LEAGUES

Worldwide links
www.debating.net

Debating Matters, UK
www.debatingmatters.com

Auckland Debating Society, New Zealand
www.ada.org.nz/schlevels.php

Debaters Association of Victoria, Australia
www.debating.netspace.net.au

Index

Acknowledgements

Photo credits: Digital Vision: 11, 19, 30, 37. Ecoscene/ Stephen Coyne: 15. © Bruce Davidson/naturepl.com: 16. Photo Disc: 42-43. Action Press/Rex Features: 36. James Fraser/Rex Features: cover, 28. Frank Siteman/Rex Features: 32. Mauro Fermariello/Science Photo Library: 26. S. Chamnanrith/UNEP/Still Pictures: 8. Mark Edwards/Still Pictures: 35. Nicolas Granier/Still Pictures: 24. Mike Powles/WWI/Still Pictures: 23. UNEP/Still Pictures: 38. Jim Wark/Still Pictures: 20, 40. TopFoto: 12-13. TopFoto/ Imageworks: 4-5, 6, 18.

Text acknowledgements: P6: 1 Richard Mackay, *The Penguin Atlas of Endangered Species: A Worldwide Guide to Plants and Animals*, Penguin, 2002; 2 Stephen Budiansky, *Nature's Keepers*, New York: Free Press, 1995; 3 Bjorn Lomborg, *The Skeptical Environmentalist: Measuring the Real State of the World*, CUP, 2001; P7: 1 Tom Lovejoy, 'Biodiversity', Reith Lecture 2000: http://news.bbc.co.uk/hi/english/static/events/reith_2000/lecture2.stm (20.06.05); 2 Stuart Pimm, 'The Sixth Extinction', *National Geographic*, February 1999; 3 Durrell Wildlife: http://www.durrellwildlife.org/index.cfm?a=94 (20.06.05); P8: 1 Colin Tudge, *The Variety of Life: A Survey and a Celebration of All the Creatures That Have Ever Lived*, OUP, 2002; 2 'Conservation of Biological Diversity', Chapter 15, Agenda 21: http://www.un.org/esa/sustdev/documents/agenda21/english/agenda21chapter15.htm (20.06.05); 3 Chief Seattle, 19th Century Native American in a letter to President Pierce (unsubstantiated); 4 Edward O. Wilson, et al *The Diversity of Life*, Penguin, 2001; P9: 1 Lord May, 'Science, the Natural World and Public Opinion: Are We in Crisis?' Speaking at The Natural History Museum, London quoted on: http://www.fathom.com/feature/190137/ (20.06.05); 2 Montsanto Biotech Primer website: http://www.monsanto.co.uk/primer/benefits.html (20.06.05); 3 World Conservation Monitoring Centre, 'Biodiversity: An Overview', December 1995, quoted on http://www.life.uiuc.edu/bio100/lectures/s97lects/20Biodiversity/WCM.html; P10: 1 Brad Smith, quoted in, 'Forests return; future uncertain', *Michigan News*, February 17, 2005; 2 President George W Bush at Signing of H.R. 1904, the Healthy Forests Restoration Act of 2003, US Department of Agriculture, Washington, D.C.: http://www.whitehouse.gov/news/releases/2003/12/20031203-4.html (21.06.05); P11: 1 Friends of the Earth: http://www.foe.co.uk/campaigns/biodiversity/issues/disappearing_forests/ (21.06.05); 2 Greenpeace International: http://www.greenpeace.org/international/news/the-forest-house (21.06.05); P12: 1 Honey, M, *Ecotourism and Sustainable Development: Who Owns Paradise?*, Washington, DC: Island Press, 1999; 2 World Wildlife Fund: http://www.wwf.org.uk/researcher/issues/Tourism/0000000171.asp (21.06.05) 3 Anon, Asia 4 Anita Roddick in a foreward to 'World's Apart' report for Tearfund, 2002; P13: UN General Assembly and UN Division for Sustainable Development, 'Sustainable Tourism. Decision of the General Assembly and the Commission on Sustainable Development: Decision 7/3. Tourism and sustainable development'; P14: 1 Wendy Vanasselt, 'Ecotourism and Conservation: Are They Compatible?' *World Resources*, 2000-2001: http://earthtrends.wri.org/text/biodiversity-protected/feature-29.html (21.06.05); American Society of Travel Agents: http://www.astanet.com/about/environmentalawards.asp (21.06.05); 3 http://www.world-tourism.org/newsroom/campaign/Tourism_enriches.pdf (21.06.05); 4 International Association of Antarctic Tour Operators: http://www.iaato.org/docs/PressRelease04-05.pdf (21.06.05); P15: 1 Convention for Biological Diversity: http://www.biodiv.org/programmes/socio-eco/tourism/default.asp (21.06.05); 2 Colin Tudge, *The Variety of Life: A Survey and a Celebration of All the Creatures That Have Ever Lived*, OUP, 2002; P16: 1 Klaus Toepfer, UNEP Executive Director, 26th November 2003: http://www.globio.info/press/2003-11-26.cfm (21.06.05); 2 Stefan Gossling, 'Ecotourism: A Means to Safeguard Biodiversity and Ecosystem Functions?' *Ecological Economics*, 29(2), May 1999, pages 303-20; P17: 1 Liz Williamson, 'Mountain Gorilla Tourism: Some Costs and Benefits', *Gorilla Journal* 22, June 2001; 2 Jaco Homsy, 'Ape Tourism and Human Diseases: How Close Should We Get?' Report of a consultancy for the International Gorilla Programme, February 1999; P18: 1 Caroline Taylor, 'The Challenge of African Elephant Conservation', Conservation Issues, April 1997; 2 Mavuso Msimang, quoted in News 24.com, 24/10/2002: http://www.wheels24.co.za/News24/South_Africa/0,,2-7_1275932,00.html (21.06.05); P19: 1 Paula Kahumba, quoted in NationalGeographic.com: http://news.nationalgeographic.com/news/2002/11/1106_021106_TVIvory_2.html (21.06.05); 2 Daphne Sheldrick, quoted in NationalGeographic.com: http://news.nationalgeographic.com/news/2002/11/1114_021114_TVIvoryTrade.html (21.06.05); 3 Richard Leakey, 'A poachers' charter: Allowing "sustainable trade" in endangered species would make a few dealers rich, while wiping out Africa's wildlife', *The Guardian*, October 7, 2004; P21: 1 Crowley, P, Fischer, H & Devonshire, A: 'Feed the World', *Chemistry in Britain*, July 1998, p25, cited in Dinham B, 1999, Zeneca the impact of pesticides on food security. Hungry for Power: UK Food Group, London, p73; 2 National Farmers' Union: http://www.nfu.org.uk/intradoc-cgi/idc_cgi_isapi.dll?IdcService=GET_DOC_PAGE&Action=GetTemplatePage&Page=NFU_ABOUT_AG_PAGE (22.06.05); 3 Séan Rickard quoted in 'Intensive farming debates: Why is there such opposition to modern farming techniques?' by Brendan O'Neill: http://www.spiked-online.com/Printable/000000005542.htm (22.06.05); 4 From a presentation made by Louise O. Fresco, Assistant Director-General, Agriculture Department, Food and Agriculture Organisation of the United Nations, to the OECD Working Group on Pesticides, Paris, 4 February 2002; P22: 1 Professor James Lovelock: http://news.bbc.co.uk/1/low/sci/tech/3766831.stm (22.06.05); 2 Lucy Siegle, 'Miss Piggy', *The Observer magazine*, 17 October 2004; 3 Colin Tudge, *So Shall We Reap*, Penguin, 2004; 4 Gregory Mock, 'Domesticating the World: Conversion of natural Ecosystems, *World Resources* 2000–2001, September 2000; P24: Mark Sagoff, 'What's Wrong with Exotic Species?', Institute for Philosophy and Public Policy: http://www.puaf.umd.edu/IPPP/fall1999/exotic_species.htm (22.06.05); 3 'New flora and fauna for old', *The Economist*, 21 December 2000; 4 FIGIS: http://www.fao.org/figis/servlet/FiRefServlet?ds=topic&fid=13532 (22.06.05); P25: 1 World Resources Institute 2000, quoted in 'Protecting Ecosystems in a Changing World' by Jessica Forrest, July 2003; 2 Jeffrey A. McNeely, 'The great reshuffling: How alien species help feed the global economy' The World Conservation Union: http://www.iucn.org/biodiversityday/mcneelyreshuffling.html (22.06.05); 3 'The basics on alien invasive species', The World Conservation Union: http://www.iucn.org/biodiversityday/overview.html (22.06.05); P26: 1 Oliver A. Ryder, *Trends in Biotechnology*, 2002, vol 20, 231-232; 2 'Dr Robert Lanza quoted in: 'Cloning An Endangered Species', CBS News, October 8 2000: http://www.cbsnews.com/stories/2000/10/08/tech/main239486.shtml (22.06.05) 3 Dr. David Faber, quoted in 'Collaborative Effort Yields Endangered Species Clone': http://www.advancedcell.com/2003-04-08.htm (22.06.05); P27: 1 Malcom Tait, 'Bessie And The Gaur – cloning of endangered or extinct species is not legitimate wildlife conservation', *The Ecologist*, December 2000; 2 Micheal Novacek quoted in: 'Cloning An Endangered Species', CBS News, October 8 2000: http://www.cbsnews.com/stories/2000/10/08/tech/main239486.shtml (22.06.05); 3 Belinda Wright quoted in 'Cloning Breeds Hope for India's Big Cats', *The Guardian*, 17th August 2004; P28: 1 National Organisation to Abolish Zoos: http://www.noazark.org/myths/Index.htm (22.06.05); 2 Richard Mackay, *The Penguin Atlas of Endangered Species: A Worldwide Guide to Plants and Animals*, Penguin, 2002; 3 Virginia McKenna: http://www.bornfree.org.uk/zoocheck/index.html (22.06.05); 4 Colin Tudge, *The Variety of Life: A Survey and a Celebration of All the Creatures That Have Ever Lived*, OUP, 2002; P29: 1 Barry Kent MacKay, 'When Captive Breeding Works' Mainstream, Volume 25, Number 4, Winter 1994; 2 WWF, 'Zoos and Captive Breeding': http://www.panda.org/news_facts/education/high_school/conservation_issues/consdetails.cfm?consID=2 (22.06.05); 3 Wildlife Conservation Society: http://www.wcs.org/ (22.06.05); P30: 1 http://www.bbc.co.uk/nature/environment/conservationnow/global/forests/page2.shtml; 2 Valli Moosa, quoted in 'New World Conservation Boss Eyes Climate, Oceans', 26 November 2004: http://www.earthdive.com/front_end/news/newsdetail.asp?id=820 (22.06.05); P31: 1 Bjorn Lomborg, *The Skeptical Environmentalist: Measuring the Real State of the World*, CUP, 2001; 2 Myron Ebell, quoted in 'Beckett upbeat on climate change', BBC News, 4 November 2004: http://news.bbc.co.uk/1/hi/uk_politics/3981613.stm (22.06.05); 3 George W Bush, 'President Bush Discusses Global Climate Change', Whitehouse Office of the Press Secretary June 11, 2001: http://www.whitehouse.gov/news/releases/2001/06/20010611-2.html; P32: 1 The Network of Women Ministers of the Environment, quoted in 'A Unique Voice', by Laura Liswood: http://www.ourplanet.com/imgversn/152/liswood.html; 2 Fred Pearce, 'People versus nature', *New Scientist*, 8th May 2001; P33: 1 Bjorn Lomborg, *The Skeptical Environmentalist*: Measuring the Real State of the World, CUP, 2001; 2 Nitin Desai quoted in 'A commitment to sustainable development', World Summit on Sustainable Development, August 26, 2002: http://www.chico.mweb.co.za/za/archive/2002aug/26aug-commitment.html (22.06.05); P34: 1 Tony Blair, quoted in House of Commons Environmental Audit Committee, World Summit on Sustainable Development 2002: http://www.publications.parliament.uk/pa/cm200203/cmselect/cmenvaud/98/98.pdf; 2 Professor Raven, Fifth Darwin Initiative Lecture, 21 May 2003, 'Our Choice: How Many Species Will Survive the 21st Century'; 3 Vandana Shiva: http://www.yale.edu/edsig/shiva.html (22.06.05); P35: 1 Antonio La Vina, Gretchen Hoff, and Anne Marie DeRose, World Resources Institute Working Paper 'The Success and Failure of Johannesburg: A Story of Many Summits', June 2003; 2 Jonathon Porritt, 'Do we really care enough to save ourselves?' *The Guardian*, 22 August 2002; P36: 1 Sverrir Haukur Gunnlaugsson quoted in 'WDCS responds to Iceland's justifications for its whaling programme' Whale and Dolphin Conservation Society: http://www.wdcs.org/dan/publishing.nsf/allweb/BE2BFF61C6BD258E80256F3500551530 (22.06.05); 2 Joji Morishita, *The Ecologist*; P37: 1 http://www.bbc.co.uk/nature/environment/conservationnow/global/marine/page2.shtml (22.06.05); 2 Bob Holmes, *New Scientist*, 17 May 2004; P38: 1 David White quoted in Miami Herald 15th November 2004; 2 Earthdive.com, November 2004: http://www.earthdive.com/front_end/news/default.asp?month=11&changedate=true&changeyear=2004 (22.06.05); 3 Mark D. Spalding, Corinna Ravilious, Edmund P. Green, United Nations Environment Programme (Corporate Author), World Conservation Monitoring Centre (Corporate Author) *World Atlas of Coral Reefs*, University of California Press, 2001; P39: 1 ICRAN (International Coral Reef Action Network): http://www.icran.org/cadre6.htm (22.06.05); 2 Caspar Henderson, 'Coral decline', *The Ecologist*, 22/01/2001; 3 Klaus Toepfer quoted in: http://www.unep-wcmc.org/marine/coralatlas/PRESs_RELEASE.htm (22.06.05); P40: 1 Jiang Zemin, Speech Marking Yangtze-Damming for Three Gorges Project, November 8, 1997: http://www.chinaembassy.org.nz/eng/zt/sxgc/t39462.htm (22.06.05); 2 Hydro research foundation: www.hydrofoundation.org; 3 The World bank Group: http://lnweb18.worldbank.org/ESSD/ardext.nsf/18ByDocName/SectorsandThemesDamsandReservoirs (22.06.05); P41: James Wolfensohn, 'Dammed if you do', *The Economist*, 23 September 2004; 2 Probe International: www.probeinternational.org; 3 World Commission on Dams: http://www.irn.org/wcd/ (22.06.05); P42: 1 Gerald Durrell: http://www.durrellwildlife.org/index.cfm?a=94 (22.06.05); 2 Question & Answer Discussion with Prof. Wangari Maathai November 12, 2004: http://gbmna.org/a.php?id=27&t=p.